GPjc
03-07

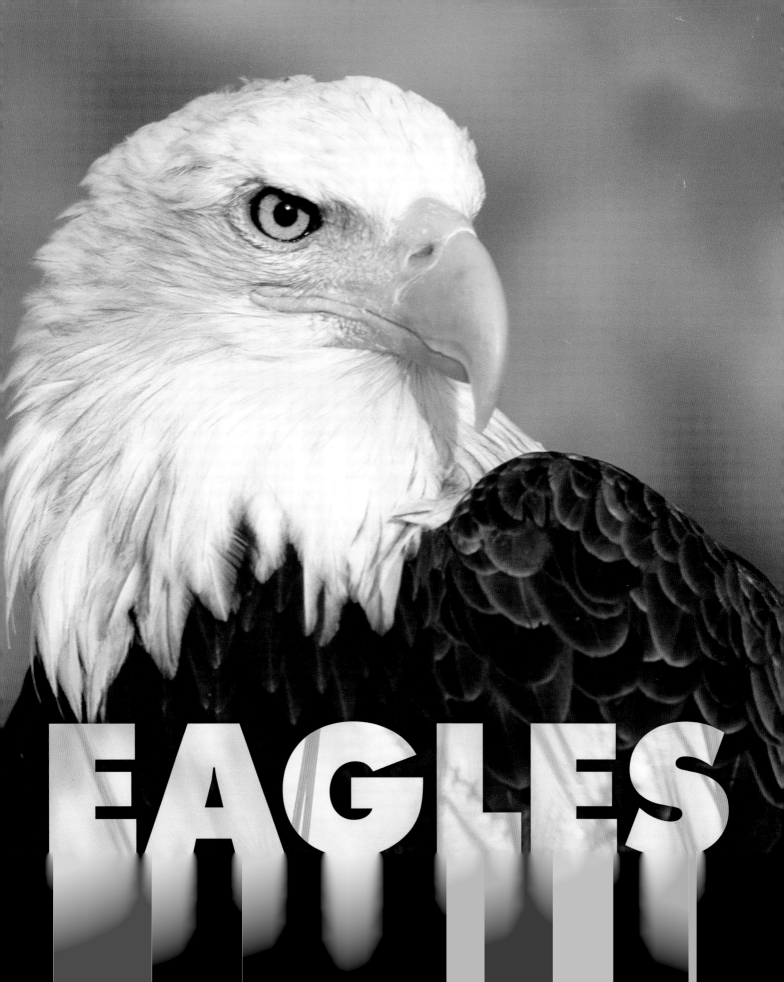

EAGLES

The Child's World

Content Adviser:
The Zoological Society
of San Diego

Published in the United States of America by The Child's World®
PO Box 326 • Chanhassen, MN 55317-0326
800-599-READ • www.childsworld.com

PHOTO CREDITS

© Daniel J. Cox/naturalexposures.com: 28–29
© Dominique Braud/Dembinsky Photo Associates: 22–23
© Frank Lane Picture Agency/Corbis: 10
© Joe McDonald: 5, 16–17, 19
© Kennan Ward/Corbis: 7
© Mark J. Thomas/Dembinsky Photo Associates: 8–9
© Peter Johnson/Corbis: 14–15
© Richard Hamilton Smith/Corbis: 25
© Robert and Linda Mitchell: 20
© Roy Toft/Getty Images: 13
© Tim Laman/Getty Images: 26–27
© Tom Murphy/Getty Images: 21
© W. Perry Conway/Corbis: cover, 1

ACKNOWLEDGMENTS

The Child's World®: Mary Berendes, Publishing Director;
Katherine Stevenson, Editor

The Design Lab: Kathleen Petelinsek, Design and Page Production

LIBRARY OF CONGRESS CATALOGING-IN-PUBLICATION DATA

Merrick, Patrick.
  Eagles / by Patrick Merrick.
    p. cm. — (New naturebooks)
  Includes bibliographical references and index.
  ISBN 1-59296-636-5 (library bound : alk. paper)
  1. Eagles—Juvenile literature. I. Title. II. Series.
  QL696.F32M48 2006
  598.9'42—dc22   2006001364

Table of Contents

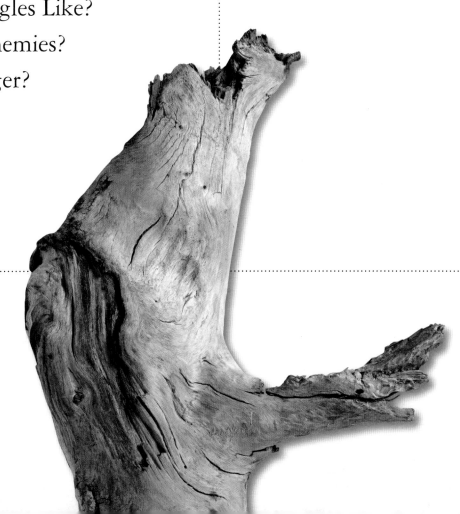

On the cover: This bald eagle is watching its surroundings on a bright autumn day.

Meet the Eagle!

As the sun moves high across the sky, the forest stays shady and quiet. A rabbit carefully sniffs the air and hops into a clearing. As the rabbit begins to munch on some tender leaves, a shadow suddenly appears. A giant bird glides toward the rabbit. Quickly, the bird folds its wings and dives downward. Just as the rabbit tries to hop away, the huge bird picks it up with its sharp claws. What type of bird is this? It's an eagle!

This golden eagle is feeding on a rabbit in Utah. Golden eagles have long been thought of as symbols of strength and power because of their large size—they can grow to be 3 feet (1 m) from beak to tail. These eagles are common in the mountain areas of the western United States and Canada.

What Do Eagles Look Like?

Bald eagles were named for their white head, neck, and tail feathers. When these eagles were named many years ago, the word "balde" meant "white."

***Bateleur* means "tumbler" or "tight-rope walker" in French. It's thought that Bateleur eagles got their name because they rock and tilt in the air the way a tightrope walker might.**

Eagles belong to a group of birds called **raptors**. Raptors are birds that hunt and eat other animals. The animals they eat are called their **prey**. Eagles are built for hunting. They have small, slim bodies and large, rounded wings. The large wings help the eagles soar above the ground as they search for food.

Eagles are covered with long feathers. Most eagle feathers are brown, black, white, or grey. All eagles have curved beaks to help them hold and tear apart their food. And all eagles have incredibly strong feet with sharp claws, or **talons**. Without their powerful feet, eagles would not be able to hold, catch, or kill the animals they hunt.

Bateleur eagles like this one live in Africa. Bateleurs have very short tails—their legs stick out past their tails when they fly! Unlike most eagles, Bateleur eagles have some patches of bright color.

Where Do Eagles Live?

Bald eagles live throughout much of North America. They live in every U.S. state except Hawai'i.

Eagles have been around for millions of years. They live in every part of the world except Antarctica. Eagles need large areas in which to live and hunt. They can be found in many different **habitats**—in deserts, jungles, mountains, and plains.

This bald eagle has just snatched a fish out of an Alaskan river. Bald eagles grow to be about 3 feet (1 m) long and weigh about 11 pounds (5 kg). These graceful birds live as far north as Alaska and as far south as Florida.

Once a pair of eagles finds a safe place, they begin to build a huge nest called an **aerie**. Most aeries are built very high up—either on cliffs or in treetops. Eagles usually return to the same nest every year, and every year they add on to the nest. Since eagles can live for 40 years, their nests can grow to be huge. One nest in Ohio was used for 36 years and weighed almost 2,000 pounds (907 kg)!

Eagles that live in forests have short wings and longer tails. This helps them turn easily as they chase their food through trees and branches. Eagles that search for animals by soaring up in the sky have longer, broader wings.

This bald eagle's aerie is high above Canada's Great Slave Lake. You can see two bald eagle chicks in the nest, waiting for their dinner.

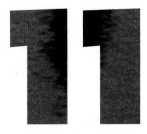

11

Are There Different Types of Eagles?

Harpy eagles have legs as thick as a person's wrist. Their talons can be as big as those of a grizzly bear!

There are more than 50 different types, or **species**, of eagles. Some, like the Ayre's hawk-eagle, are fairly small. Ayre's hawk-eagles are only 16 inches (41 cm) long and weigh only two pounds (1 kg). Others, like the giant harpy eagle, are three feet (1 m) long and weigh 20 pounds (9 kg)! Harpy eagles also have a huge **wingspan**—the distance from wingtip to wingtip. When their wings are outstretched, an adult harpy eagle's wingspan can reach seven feet (2 m)!

Harpy eagles like this one live in the forests of Central and South America. Despite their huge size, these eagles are fast fliers. Their powerful wings and strong feet allow them to pluck up animals as large as 17 pounds (8 kg)! Harpy eagles are very rare and are now protected in many areas.

Even though there are lots of different kinds of eagles, they all belong to one of two basic types: sea eagles and land eagles. Sea eagles have bare legs with rough scales on the bottoms of their feet. The scales help them hold onto the slippery fish they like to eat. Land eagles have feathers all the way down to their feet. These leg feathers make land eagles look as if they are wearing boots!

Bald eagles, Steller's sea eagles, and African fish eagles are all types of sea eagles.

Golden eagles, wedge-tailed eagles, and martial eagles are all types of land eagles.

Tawny eagles like this one live in Africa. They grow to be about 2 feet (almost 1 m) long and have wingspans of up to 6 feet (2 m). Look at the feathers on this eagle's legs. Is it a sea eagle or a land eagle?

15

What Do Eagles Eat?

Harpy eagles are known as the "jaguars of the air" because they are able to sneak up on their prey and pluck it from the treetops.

Some people claim to have seen hungry golden eagles eating turtles. How? They say the eagles drop the turtles from great heights to break open the shells.

Eagles are meat-eating **predators**. They eat everything from insects and fish to rabbits and birds. Some eagles have been known to eat snakes, too. Other eagles eat larger animals such as monkeys and young deer. In addition to live food, eagles eat **carrion**, or dead animals. And some eagles in city areas will even pick through trash in search of a meal!

This martial eagle is feeding on a young gazelle it just killed in Kenya. Martial eagles live in Africa and can be almost 3 feet (1 m) long and weigh up to 14 pounds (6 kg).

How Do Eagles Hunt?

Wedge-tailed eagles of Australia sometimes hunt in groups. By working together, these eagles can kill animals as large as adult kangaroos.

Some eagles, such as bald eagles, eat mostly fish. They snatch fish that swim too close to the surface, plucking them out of the water with their strong feet.

Eagles usually hunt from the air. With their huge wings, these birds fly wonderfully well. They can glide as fast as 50 miles (80 kg) per hour and soar as high as 7,000 feet (2,134 m). When eagles fly that high, people on the ground cannot even see them. But eagles have much better eyesight than people. In fact, they can spot a tiny mouse from 1,000 feet (305 m) up!

Once an eagle sees its victim, it folds its wings close to its body. Folding its wings causes it to drop quickly toward the ground. When the eagle reaches its prey, it uses its powerful feet to grab the animal. It kills the animal by squeezing it, then carries it off to its nest.

This bald eagle is about to catch a fish that is swimming just under the water's surface. Can you see how its talons are ready to strike?

How Are Baby Eagles Born?

Eagle eggs are just a little bigger than chicken eggs.

Eagle chicks often fight each other for food. The stronger chicks push themselves toward their parents and try to get more food than their brothers and sisters.

When a male eagle is about four years old, he begins to look for a mate. He does this by calling to a female and doing flying stunts in the air. Eagles mate for life. Soon after mating, the female lays up to three eggs.

Eagles are very good parents. Both the male and the female sit on the eggs and protect them from danger. After about 40 days, the eggs are ready to hatch. Each baby eagle breaks through its egg by tapping on it with a special bump on its beak. It might take the baby eagle more than 30 hours to break out of its shell!

20

Here you can see a golden eagle chick as it begins to break out of its egg. Opposite page: These two bald eagle chicks (one is curled up behind the other) are sitting in their aerie in Alaska.

What Are Baby Eagles Like?

Another name for a baby eagle is an *eaglet*.

If threatened, eaglets lie as flat as they can in the nest.

Eaglets learn to fly when they are about two months old. They usually leave the nest when they are about six months old.

Baby eagles are very small when they first hatch. They are also very hungry. In fact, baby eagles can eat almost as much as their parents! The adult eagles fly to and from the nest all day long to bring food to their growing babies. As the babies get older, the parents help them learn to fly and hunt, too. When they are ready to leave the nest, the babies fly away and find homes of their own.

Here a bald eagle parent feeds its 4-week-old chick. You can see a piece of meat strung between the parent's beak and the chick's.

Do Eagles Have Enemies?

Before the 1970s, a chemical called DDT was used to kill bugs in the United States. DDT often washed into rivers and lakes where bald eagles caught fish to eat. The DDT made the eagles' eggshells very thin. The numbers of baby eagles dropped. In fact, bald eagles were in danger of dying out! Today, it is illegal to use DDT in the U.S., and bald eagles have begun to make a comeback.

Eagles don't have very many enemies. They are too big and fly too fast for many animals to try to catch them. Their only real enemy is people. When we build cities and roads in the areas where eagles live, we destroy their habitats. We also harm the animals eagles need to hunt for food. To save eagles, we must protect the places where they live.

This bald eagle is resting on a pile of trash in Alaska. Eagles that live near towns often hunt in or near garbage dumps and trash piles. They eat bits of food they find in the piles, as well as any bugs and mice feeding on the garbage.

Are Eagles in Danger?

The Madagascar fish eagle is one of the rarest birds in the world—there are only about 250 left.

The endangered Philippine eagle is the national bird of the Philippines.

Many species of eagles are **endangered**. That means there are so few left in the wild, they might die out completely. Because eagles are in such danger, many countries are working to save them. These countries have set up special areas where eagles can live safely. Many other countries are working to stop the pollution that destroys the eagles' food.

26

Philippine eagles live only in the Philippine Islands. People also call these rare eagles "monkey-eating eagles" because small monkeys are one of their favorite foods.

Few animals are as fierce or as beautiful as the eagle. We are lucky to have the chance to see them. By reducing pollution and protecting eagles' habitats, we are slowly helping these wonderful birds make a comeback. Through hard work and saving the eagles' homes, people will be able to see eagles in the wild for many years to come.

Depending on the species, eagles make a number of different sounds. Most eagles scream, but others can also click, whistle, and even quack.

If they accidentally land in the water, bald eagles move their wings in a motion a little like the "butterfly" swimming stroke. This helps them stay afloat long enough to reach the shore.

Seeing a bald eagle soar high overhead is a beautiful sight! This adult is carrying a fish back to its Alaskan nest.

29

Glossary

aerie (AIR-ee) An aerie is a name for an eagle's nest. Some aeries are huge.

carrion (KAYR-ree-un) Carrion is dead animals. Eagles sometimes eat carrion if they cannot find fresh meat to eat.

endangered (en–DANE–jerd) When a type of animal is endangered, it is in danger of dying out. Some types of eagles are endangered.

habitat (HA–bih–tat) Habitat is the type of place or environment where an animal lives. Eagles live in a wide range of habitats.

predators (PREH-duh-terz) Predators are animals that hunt and kill other animals for food. Eagles are predators.

prey (PRAY) A prey animal is one that is hunted as food. Mice, rabbits, fish, and insects are all prey for eagles.

raptors (RAP–terz) Raptors are birds that hunt and eat other animals. Eagles are raptors.

species (SPEE–sheez) A species is a type of an animal. There are more than fifty different species of eagles in the world.

talons (TAL–unz) Talons are the claws on an eagle's feet. The eagle uses its talons to kill its prey and carry it off.

wingspan (WING-span) A bird's wingspan is the distance from wingtip to wingtip when its wings are outstretched. Some eagles have huge wingspans.

To Find Out More

Read It!

Barnes, Julia. *101 Facts About Eagles*. Milwaukee, WI: Gareth Stevens, 2004.

Bernhard, Emery, and Durga Bernhard (illustrator). *Eagles: Lions of the Sky*. New York: Holiday House, 1994.

Johnson, Sylvia A., and Ron Winch (photographer). *Raptor Rescue!: An Eagle Flies Free*. New York: Dutton Children's Books, 1995.

Kops, Deborah. *Eagles and Osprey*. Woodbridge, CT: Blackbirch Press, 2000.

Parry-Jones, Jemima. *Eagle & Birds of Prey*. New York: Dorling Kindersley, 2000.

On the Web

Visit our home page for lots of links about eagles: *http://www.childsworld.com/links*

Note to Parents, Teachers, and Librarians: We routinely check our Web links to make sure they're safe, active sites—so encourage your readers to check them out!

31

Index

About the Author

When Pat Merrick was a child, his family traveled and moved many times. He became fascinated with science and finding out about the world around him. In college he majored in science and education. After, college, Mr. Merrick and his wife both decided to become teachers and try and help kids learn to love the world around them. He has taught science to all levels of kids, from kindergarten through twelfth grade. When not teaching or writing, Mr. Merrick loves to read and play with his six children. He currently lives in a small town in southern Minnesota with his wife and family.